NOW YOU KNOW
CRIME SCENES

NOW YOU KNOW CRIME SCENES

DOUG LENNOX

THE DUNDURN GROUP
TORONTO

Editor: Nigel Heseltine
Copy editor: Jennifer Gallant
Design: Alison Carr
Printer: Webcom

**Library and Archives Canada
Cataloguing in Publication**

Lennox, Doug
    Now you know crime scenes /
Doug Lennox.

ISBN 978-1-55002-774-7

    1. Forensic sciences--Miscellanea.
2. Criminal
investigation--Miscellanea. I. Title.

HV8073.L46 2007   363.25
C2007-903568-X

        1   2   3   4   5
    11   10   09   08   07

**Conseil des Arts   Canada Council
du Canada   for the Arts**

**ONTARIO ARTS COUNCIL
CONSEIL DES ARTS DE L'ONTARIO**
an Ontario government agency | un organisme du gouvernement de l'Ontario

Canadä

We acknowledge the support of
The Canada Council for the Arts
and the Ontario Arts Council for
our publishing program. We also
acknowledge the financial support
of the Government of Canada
through the Book Publishing
Industry Development Program and
The Association for the Export of
Canadian Books, and the Government
of Ontario through the Ontario Book
Publishers Tax Credit program, and
the Ontario Media Development
Corporation.

Printed and bound in Canada.
Printed on recycled paper.

www.dundurn.com

Dundurn Press
3 Church Street, Suite 500
Toronto, Ontario, Canada
M5E 1M2

Gazelle Book Services Limited
White Cross Mills
High Town, Lancaster,
England LA1 4XS

Dundurn Press
2250 Military Road
Tonawanda, NY
U.S.A. 14150

NOW YOU KNOW
CRIME SCENES

CONTENTS

PREFACE

We live in a country that has chosen to assume that a person accused of a crime is innocent until guilt is proved beyond a reasonable doubt. Most of us agree that this is honourable and right, but it does place a huge responsibility upon police and forensic investigators involved in the investigation of a crime. To achieve the high standard of proof required for a conviction, these men and women must always remember that their actions on the job have to withstand critical examination in a court of law.

This book answers questions about crime scene investigation, provides some historical context, and offers accounts of various crimes to illustrate how good investigative techniques have worked in practice.

Research has gone into every question with the aim of entertaining readers of all ages. I learned a great deal while working on this book. I hope you will, too.

CRIME SCENE RESPONSE

How did 911 get started?

Canada began to provide 911 services in 1972. AT&T introduced the service in the United States in 1968. Britain was well ahead. They began a 999 service in 1937 following a terrible fire in London in 1935 that led to the deaths of five people.

What happens when you call 911?

Dispatch asks whether you need police, fire department, ambulance, or all the above. They try to get your location, particularly if you are on a cellphone and your location can't be pinpointed automatically. You will have to describe the problem, say who is hurt, and how badly. If it is safe for you to keep talking, more questions will seek to calm you or help the emergency workers prepare for their arrival at the scene.

What is the responding officer's responsibility at the crime scene?

A preliminary investigation begins when police officers are dispatched on a call. On the way, they plan their response. At the crime scene, they start by helping the injured, chasing suspects, gathering witnesses, trying to determine if a crime was actually committed, and requesting appropriate backup from headquarters. As soon as possible, they secure the crime scene and locate or collect evidence. They take good notes throughout. Although the reality of most crime scenes makes achieving all these objectives difficult, the better this work is done, the better the chance the criminals will be caught and convicted.

What is a crime scene?

The preliminary investigating officer makes the first attempt at defining the crime scene by running tape around its perimeter to stop people removing or contaminating evidence. Crime scenes may be as small as the room of a house or as large as a park, and some crimes may have several crime scenes. As more is learned about the crime, the crime scene may be enlarged or reduced.

Do the police draw chalk lines around a body?

Lines, tape, paint, and ropes have all been used to mark the location of a body, especially if it was going to be moved. However, the practice is risky because of the chance of evidence contamination. Often the coordinates of the body are established by measuring to it from known fixed points and by taking photographs.

What are solvability factors?

Police resources are spread thin, so many crimes get little attention, and some get almost none at all. One factor used to determine whether police will spend time on a case is its solvability as determined by the preliminary investigating officer, the one who responded to the call. Crimes become solvable when there are witnesses, good information about the suspect, good physical evidence, and identifiable property. If these factors are not present, the case will probably be closed or suspended.

Why is it important for investigators to take notes?

Memories are unreliable, more and more so as time passes. That is why courts prefer physical evidence or testimony supported by notes. Good note taking can save constables and detectives embarrassment in court. As well as containing names of victims, witnesses, and suspects, good notes describe important details of the crime scene, such as bullet holes or broken lamps, the locations of key pieces of evidence, and the things people say and their behaviour in the heat of the moment.

What goes into a preliminary investigation report?

These reports are usually largely checklists. They contain information like the case number; the officer's badge number; time, date, and location of the crime; limited personal information about victims, suspects, and witnesses; weather conditions; lighting; vehicle descriptions; crime scene description (building, car, outdoor location); means of access; and the criminal's objective.

When does the press get to know what is going on?

With good contacts within police departments, some journalists used to get the scoop quickly, feeding sensationalistic tabloid newspapers a steady stream of lurid crime drama before authorities were ready to make the details public. In recent years, getting the scoop has become more difficult. Police forces now train some staff to speak to the media and limit what anyone else can say.

Police argue that privacy considerations, the suspect's right to a fair trial, and the need to preserve evidence integrity at a crime scene make restrictions on media access necessary.

Who cleans a crime site after the removal of a body?

Perhaps the most emotionally taxing job at the crime scene is that of the trauma cleanup crews, sometimes called "death cleaners." When someone dies, bodily fluids escape, and depending on the circumstances, other human remains may be left behind. After the body is taken to the morgue, private companies are called to clean up the mess. These specialists are often former medical staff and often know something about construction as well. They enter the premises in haz-mat biohazard suits and collect the remains and anything touched by the victim, which can include walls, carpets, furniture, and more.

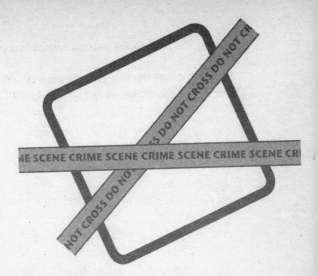

SIGNS OF CRIMES

What was the name given to the first device used to test drivers for alcohol?

As Prohibition ended in the United States, Dr. Rolla Harger, a biochemistry professor, invented the "Drunkometer." Patented in 1936, the device collected a suspect's breath in a balloon and fed it through a chemical solution. In 1954, the "Breathalyzer" was invented. Harger worked on that, too, and efforts continue to make it more accurate. Both devices have routinely faced challenge in court on grounds of unreliability and poor calibration.

Why are marijuana grow ops such a big problem?

The occurrence of frequent brownouts or power surges in a neighbourhood is an indication that a grow op may be operating there, because grow ops need large amounts of electricity to run lights and equipment. Grow up operators often hide this excess electricity consumption by illegally bypassing the meter; when they do not, electric bills can be important evidence. However, police often have difficulty getting access to the electricity bill for a suspect house because the utility has an obligation to protect the privacy of its customers. Often police must find other evidence to convince a judge that a house is probably being used to grow marijuana before the information will be released to them. This makes prosecuting grow ops much more difficult.

Neither police nor utilities are happy with this state of affairs. Police would like information on suspicious electricity use to be proactively released to them by utilities, and utilities would like to recover the millions of dollars they are losing to electricity theft. With those objectives in mind, they are developing new ways of working together, and technology, such as metering from the street, is offering ways to counter tactics used by the criminals.

Quickies

Did you know ...

- that signs a house may be a grow op include heavy use of electricity and water, condensation on the windows, lots of vents on the roof, skunky odours, windows papered over, unusual noises, kids' toys but no kids, and nobody bringing groceries to the home?

How do you tell a gunshot from a car backfire?

Car backfires are not that common these days, so the need to make the distinction is probably not as important as it used to be, which is just as well because the task is difficult. Some closed-circuit television (CCTV) cameras have software to detect the difference.

How are crooks identified using surveillance cameras?

With surveillance cameras becoming increasingly common, new ways are being sought to reliably match their images with criminal mug shots. For instance, anthropometric (human measuring) techniques are used to determine distances between facial features, like the eyes, mouth, and nose. The idea is that these measurements can be used to create a short list of potential criminals by comparing them to pictures in a mug shot database. The challenge for police is that people's faces appear at all angles in a video, and getting a straight-on shot can be difficult or impossible.

What is CompStat?

The CompStat program, which was developed in the mid-1990s, tracks crime across the city of New York, identifying emerging crime hot spots such as a specific street corner so the local precinct can focus on it and bring the illegal activity under control before it becomes a major problem. The data is updated constantly, allowing police to quickly analyze whether the latest strategy is working.

Who was the most notorious mass murderer ever convicted?

A man named Pedro Alonso Lopez claimed to have murdered more than three hundred girls (he showed Ecuadorian police the bodies of fifty-three of them) in Colombia, Ecuador, and Peru between his release from prison in 1978 and his recapture in 1980. Dubbed the "Monster of the Andes," he received a life sentence in Ecuador. By various accounts, he is thought to have died, been released at the border to Colombia, or escaped around 1998.

As bad a Pedro was, a sixteenth-century Hungarian noblewoman in Transylvania named Erzebet Bathory, "The Blood Countess," may have been worse. In 1611, she went to prison for torturing and murdering eighty girls, but a book she kept listed the names of more than six hundred.

CRIME SCENE INVESTIGATION

What are typical motives for major crimes?

A criminal can give all sorts of reasons for committing a capital crime, but generally it comes down to half a dozen possibilities: they want to kill someone, escape, hide another crime, obtain an insurance payout, put someone out of business, or get revenge.

Who were the world's first detectives?

In 1749, the Bow Street Runners were formed in London to detect and catch criminals. The noted author Henry

Fielding, who worked as a magistrate for the city, and his half-brother, John, established them to send a message to criminals that crime would not go unpunished. The runners were drawn from a notorious group of men known as "thief-takers," what we would call bounty hunters today.

Where was the world's first private detective agency?

Eugène François Vidocq, who began his career as a soldier and criminal and went on to be a spy and informant for the French police, started a detective agency called Le bureau des renseignments (Office of Intelligence) in 1834. His life and his investigative techniques provided inspiration for works by many writers, including Edgar Allan Poe, Sir Arthur Conan Doyle, and Victor Hugo. He is also credited with contributions to ballistics and criminology.

Where was North America's first private detective agency?

Allan Pinkerton started the Pinkerton National Detective Agency in Chicago in 1850, after dissolving the North-Western Police Agency, which he had created with a partner. When a Pinkerton detective uncovered a plot to assassinate Abraham Lincoln, the agency's reputation grew enormously. Later, strike-breaking work for industrialists like Andrew Carnegie in the late 1800s made many people dislike the company. Inspiration for the term "private eye" came from Pinkerton's logo, which featured an eye and the motto "We never sleep."

What does a detective write up?

A detective's paperwork is more free form than the constable's is. She uses short paragraphs to describe the crime, the work of the investigating officers, the investigation, the arrest, the interrogation, and the supplementary reports.

Who took the Mafia out of the trash-collecting business in New York?

New York police detective Rick Cowan spent years undercover during the mid-1990s as Dan Benedetto, cousin of the owner of a recycling company. He planted listening devices and wore wires to gather evidence against Mafiosi who were controlling the industry in New York. His evidence and testimony led to seventy-two convictions.

What should you wear to a crime scene?

The well-turned-out crime scene investigator should prepare for the task much as a surgeon prepares for an operation. An undistinguished disposable jumpsuit should begin the ensemble, followed by disposable booties, surgical gloves, hat, and mask. The important thing is to avoid contaminating evidence. Properly done, this outfit, called personal protective equipment (PPE), not only protects evidence, but may protect the investigator from biohazards as well.

How should the crime scene investigator accessorize?

The fully accessorized investigator ought to carry a toolkit with scalpels, haemostats, mirrors, magnets, tape to lift fingerprints, brushes, assorted powders, magnifying glasses, tweezers, index cards, inkpad, evidence seals, labels, and a ruler. She also needs various bags and bottles for containing evidence, and evidence markers for use when taking photographs.

Quickies

Did you know ...

• that J. Edgar Hoover, who died in office forty-eight years after assuming the top job at the Federal Bureau of Investigation (FBI) in 1924, denied the existence of the Mafia for most of his career?

How does an investigator do a walk-through at a crime scene?

During a walk-through, an investigator will make a first attempt to reconstruct the crime, document evidence that is going to be removed, and note ways into and out of the crime scene. She will also decide who needs to take part in the full investigation, assess the risks, and request special equipment. All the while, she will try not to disturb any areas that may contain evidence and keep her hands in her pockets or behind her back to avoid touching anything.

How did poor evidence collection help the O.J. Simpson defence?

No case in modern times has more resoundingly demonstrated the importance of good evidence handling at a crime scene. A long list of procedural errors, including several recorded on a police video of the search of Simpson's property, suggested some evidence might be tainted. One error was particularly damaging to the prosecution: an investigator handled a vial of Simpson's blood, and then bagged a leather glove found at the scene without changing his own surgical gloves, raising the possibility that cross-contamination could have occurred. The defence of course seized upon this.

What is a chain of custody log?

In the world of evidence handling, a chain of custody log is essential. Without it, there is a good chance that the evidence may be ruled inadmissible in court because no proof exists that tampering or contamination did not occur. This has become even more important in the world of computers, where it can be very easy to alter evidence, and very difficult or impossible to prove when and how changes were made. Good chain of custody procedures ensure that every time evidence is handled or moved, the people involved, the time, and the reason are recorded.

What is bagging and tagging?

Bagging and tagging is a slang phrase that describes evidence collection at a crime scene. It is the first step in the property management chain of custody process. After photography and documentation are complete, evidence should be put into clean containers — bags for dry stuff, tubes or bottles for liquids, sharps containers for hypodermic needles, paper and envelopes for pieces of hair or scrapings of blood, and biohazard bags for human or animal remains — labelled, and bagged again.

Why are film cameras still used when photographing crime scenes?

Courts trust film cameras. In addition, photographs on film can often be enlarged further, revealing details that might not show up on a digital print. Techniques like watermarking and tamperproof storage media will eventually win digital images the approval of the courts, but even without that, the sheer convenience of digital cameras means they are widely used in police and forensic work.

How is crime scene photography done?

The general area and points of entry or exit are photographed as soon as possible, to provide documentation in case evidence is moved or removed. Individual pieces of evidence are labelled, scale indicators like rulers are placed alongside, and they are photographed. Each piece gets close-up, middle distance, and long shots. Film cameras are still widely used, and images are shot in black and white as well as in colour. Digital cameras are used as well but are not generally accepted in court as evidence

Quickies
Did you know …
- that computers have opened up a world of opportunity for criminal activity, including forgery, fraud, hacking, piracy, email bombing, phishing, unauthorized access, infojacking, spying, copyright infringement, conspiracy, solicitation, backdating, keylogging, and much, much more?

because the images they produce can be easily altered in computer programs like Adobe Photoshop.

How do hackers crack passwords?

Easily. The best passwords have at least eight characters, and the characters are a random mixture of digits, symbols, and upper- and lowercase type. People do not remember passwords like these, so they make simple ones out of birthdays, cat names, and so on. That opens the digital door of a home or company to the swarms of unwelcome intruders prowling the Internet for machines they can hijack for spamming, financial information they can steal, identities they can assume, and much, much more.

What information can be collected to track someone on the Internet?

The Internet is not private or anonymous. When you go online, your machine's address can be logged, and every page you access can be recorded by the websites that you visit. Little files called cookies are deposited on the machine to allow websites to analyze your activity on their pages. Emails go to network servers before they go to a recipient's machine and can be intercepted on the way or tracked down later. The reality that you are just one of many millions using the Internet affords you the kind of protection available to individuals in a school of fish under attack from barracudas — some will survive. Beyond that, the only mechanisms giving you any semblance of privacy are standards of practice and laws that set limits on legitimate snooping by authorities.

THE SEARCH

What should an investigator remember when doing a crime scene search?

"Wherever he steps, whatever he touches, whatever he leaves will serve as a silent witness against him," wrote Edmund Locard, a French criminologist, in 1920. This statement led to the motto of forensic science, which reads, "Every contact leaves a trace." Called the Exchange Principle, this statement should be front and centre in the mind of any criminal investigator.

What are crime scene investigators looking for?

When conducting a search investigators are trying to recognize evidence and avoid everything else. Collecting too much evidence can be as bad as not collecting enough, because testing time may be wasted. When found, evidence is carefully packaged, documented, photographed, and analyzed on the spot or back at the lab.

How are crime scenes searched?

For smaller crime scenes, the most popular search technique is the inward spiral, where the investigator enters the room and carefully moves towards the centre in ever decreasing circles. This search can be conducted from the centre outwards, as well, in the event that the investigator has to go immediately to the heart of the scene to examine a victim or deal with key evidence. Other searches that are particularly useful for larger areas include the line abreast search, where everyone moves forward shoulder to shoulder, and the grid search, which involves searching an area in one direction, and then searching the same area at right angles to the original search.

What did police learn from Britain's Yorkshire Ripper case?

Peter Sutcliffe, England's Yorkshire Ripper, began his evil work in 1975, with the murder of a prostitute. After a heavily criticized five-year police investigation, he was finally caught in 1980, while in the act of carrying out what would have been his fourteenth murder. Early on, wrong assumptions were made about the identity profile of the killer, which meant Sutcliffe was interviewed nine times but did not become a suspect. In addition, so much information was gathered about the case — 250,000 people were interviewed — that nobody could get a full appreciation of it, especially since it was not stored on computer.

Crime scene searches have the following purposes:

- provide evidence of the crime (*corpus delicti*);
- show how the crime was done (*modus operendi*, or MO);
- tell what and who was at the scene;
- support or disprove witness and suspect statements;
- provide leads for solving the crime; and
- support or disprove investigative theories.

How is a shooting scene searched?

While a shooting scene will provide all kinds of evidence to consider, including blood and signs of struggle, the clues left behind by the weapon are central to solving the case. If police detained suspects, one of the first priorities is to check them for gunshot residue. At the scene, investigators collect cartridge cases and bullets and search for weapons. They also try to figure out how many shots were fired and where the shooter, or shooters, stood.

What do investigators look for to determine whether a fire was arson?

While the fire is burning, investigators will study and photograph the flames, because the colours can indicate temperature and identify what is burning — for instance, common accelerants such as gasoline create distinctive flames. Once the blaze is out, they will try to see if the place was broken into, if safety equipment like sprinklers was disabled, or if any of the odours suggest accelerants. Partially burned objects will be examined to see if they can point to where the fire began. Investigators will also want to see a reasonable quantity of valuables or stock to confirm that the place was not cleaned out before the fire started.

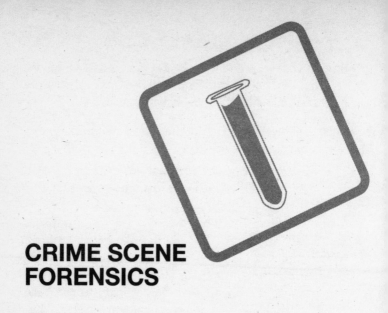

CRIME SCENE FORENSICS

Who is the evidence technician?

In many communities, evidence technicians are the forensic team's first responders. Their training in identifying, collecting, documenting, and storing the evidence found at a crime scene gives them the ability to limit the amount of evidence collected to that which will stand up in court and help solve the case. That skill is important because too much evidence can be almost as bad as too little. An investigation can be overwhelmed by the evidence and go off in wrong directions, while costs of forensic tests soar.

Why is it important to note the odours at a crime scene?

Smells can be collected at a crime scene using sterile gauze or vacuum cleaner–like devices that pull them onto a pad. Odours collected this way have been presented to dogs like bloodhounds for hundreds of years. Recently, scent helped track down the sender of several letter bombs. In another instance, an odour matched shooters to cartridges found at crime scene. A controversial case in Irvine, California, was solved when a smell from a T-shirt that had been frozen several months earlier was obtained by an odour collection device and presented to a bloodhound that then identified the suspect.

How many forensic specialists go to a crime scene?

Dozens of forensic specialties exist that might be useful at a crime scene, but it is unlikely they will all be available in any police department, no matter how big. Besides, there are just too many crimes and too few crime scene investigators. Forensic specialists will of course be out in force at major crimes, but their numbers and levels of specialization quickly diminish with the reduced severity of the crime.

Why are sketch artists still useful at the crime scene?

Sketch artists can take a description provided by the victim of a crime and draw a picture of the suspect. They can also draw pictures from descriptions of missing evidence and quickly sketch the crime scene in ways that are impossible to capture with a camera.

How are bomb scenes investigated?

On arriving at the scene, the first thing police have to do is assess the risks, call in backup, and attend to the victims, all the while being on the lookout for additional bombs. Next, a command post is set up and the area where shrapnel and debris exist is secured and measured. Investigators then do a shoulder-to-shoulder search collecting any evidence they find. Finally, using clean or sterile tools, they sweep the remaining debris into piles in the centre and sift through it.

How do airbags help determine who was behind the wheel during an accident?

When airbags deploy, they can pick up fibres, makeup, and hair from the people they protect, and leave behind bruises, lubricant, and burn marks from the hot propellant. Burn marks are particularly useful to investigators, because they appear in predictable spots on a person's body depending on whether they were caused by a driver or passenger side airbag.

What can an investigator learn from a computer?

A hard drive can be a treasure trove for a forensic team. Temporary files and paging files are an obvious target, revealing recently edited documents, whether the file still exists or not. Original files do not disappear after deletion either, even if the recycle bin has been emptied. Index files and logs are additional sources of evidence. In short, criminals need to think twice before using a computer because it can be a compelling witness for the prosecution.

When governments and corporations destroy hard drives that contain sensitive data, they do not just clean them, they obliterate them.

What is the first thing done to a body at the crime scene?

If the death is thought to have occurred shortly before police arrived at the scene, the first step is to check for signs of life and attempt to resuscitate the victim. Otherwise, the body should be approached cautiously, avoiding and making note of any evidence seen on the way.

Once beside the body, the death investigator looks at it without touching, trying to pinpoint evidence, locate wounds and injuries, and look for blood. She checks clothing, if it is present, to look for indications that the body has been moved. She also makes a sketch and takes pictures.

How is the deceased removed from a crime scene?

Requirements vary by jurisdiction, but generally, the death investigator, who will often also be a pathologist, medical examiner, or coroner, needs to confirm that death has occurred. Photographs are taken and the body's location is marked before it is moved. The investigator also looks for signs that point to time of death; wounds, bruises, and broken bones; and physical evidence that may be useful to the investigation. As soon as possible, the body is sent to the morgue for an autopsy.

ELUSIVE TRUTH

How do police handle witnesses?

When police identify someone as a witness, they ask the person to step aside, avoid talking to anyone, and remain at the scene. As soon as they get a chance, they take a statement that includes contact information and a description of the incident. The witness may also be asked to go to the station for further questioning. Later the witness may have to appear in court.

Being a witness can be stressful and may even bring threats from suspects, the accused, or their friends and families. To help witnesses cope with these realities, support groups are becoming more common. In extreme circumstances, witnesses may seek help from a range of witness protection programs.

Why did Sicily crack down on the Mafia in the mid-1990s?

Falcone-Borsellino Airport in Palermo, Sicily, is named after two Italian judges, Giovanni Falcone and Paolo Borsellino, who bravely and aggressively went after the Mafia in the 1980s. They, Falcone's wife, and many co-workers paid for the investigation with their lives in two savage bomb attacks. Public outrage following the bombings forced government to take action against organized crime.

Who was the "canary who could sing but couldn't fly"?

Informers are an important part of police work, but turning on people you used to call friends can be a dangerous business. Abraham "Kid Twist" Reles was the most feared hit man in a predominantly Jewish gang of hit men called Murder Incorporated. They killed people that Italian mobsters like Al Capone wanted out the picture during the 1930s. Reles testified against his former gang and shortly thereafter died in police custody by falling out of a window.

How are witnesses protected from intimidation?

It can take a lot of courage to be a witness at a major trial. Key witnesses in the Air India case complained of intimidation, and one prospective witness, Tara Singh Hayer, was the victim of a so far unsolved murder before he could give evidence. Recognizing the difficulties people face when they have to testify, the International Criminal Court has pushed for the establishment of "Victims and Witnesses Units" to provide counselling and support.

Witness protection is a surprisingly new enterprise. The RCMP did not have a formal witness protection program until 1984, which, after numerous complaints, was revamped under the Witness Protection Program Act of 1996. Witnesses have to qualify to be part of this program.

How good are eyewitnesses?

The Harris-Adams case of 1976 drew a stark picture of the potential unreliability of eyewitnesses. David Harris was driving a stolen car and had picked up a drifter named Randall Dale Adams near Dallas, Texas. During a routine traffic stop, an officer approached the car and was shot and killed by the driver, who then sped off. The officer's partner did not get a good look at the people in the car, but three eyewitnesses said the driver had long hair and a moustache. Initially, Harris was arrested for the crime,

41

but the witnesses' statements pointed to Adams, who was arrested instead. Harris's testimony against Adams, combined with the testimony of the witnesses, who were never cross-examined, led to Adams's conviction. Twelve years later, Adams was freed when Harris, on death row for another murder, finally admitted to the crime.

How did lineups ruin a young man's life?

One of the first court decisions overturned by DNA evidence in the United States was a guilty verdict against a man named Ronald Cotton, who received life plus fifty-four years for raping two women in North Carolina. One victim had selected him from a photo lineup and a physical lineup and remained convinced he was the rapist until DNA tests cleared him in 1995. By then he had spent eleven years in jail. Meanwhile, the DNA of another man, in jail for other crimes, who had previously claimed he committed both rapes, was found to be a match.

What are mug shots?

The first mug shots appeared on "Wanted" posters pinned up by Pinkerton men in the late 1800s. Typically, mug shots are head-on and profile views of the subject, traditionally in black and white but nowadays in colour. In recent years, new technologies have appeared that make three-dimensional mug shots in seconds.

Why can lineups and mug shots be worse than no information at all?

Mug shot presentations, or lineups, can lead to misidentifications if not done properly, resulting in arrests and even convictions of innocent people. Critics argue that mug shots or lineup participants should be shown to the witness one at time, instead of all at once. They also argue that great care must be taken not to lead the witness.

How do lie detectors work?

Lie detectors do not detect lies; they detect symptoms of lies. Their other name, polygraph, came about because their many (poly) sensors record their findings on graph paper. Lie detectors monitor breathing, pulse, blood pressure, and perspiration. John Larson, a medical student at the University of California, built the first one, which received widespread use, in 1921.

Why is lie detector evidence not admissible in court?

John Larson's invention of a lie detector quickly prompted challenges to its ability to make a reliable assessment of a subject's honesty. It was found that drugs, alcohol, hunger, pathological lying, and self-inflicted pain could all fool the machine, and incompetent operators messed things up as well. As a result, by 1923, American courts were not allowing lie detector evidence. Even with these problems, many suspects confess if they fail a test, making the detectors useful tools for the police.

How are new technologies attempting to get around the lie detector's shortcomings?

The search for something to do a better job of identifying liars has been ongoing almost since the first polygraph. Lately some new technologies have been showing promise. Electroencephalograms look for specific brainwaves that change when the subject lies. Magnetic resonance imaging reveals a lie when certain parts of the brain become well oxygenated. Eye scans capitalize on the fact that extra blood flows to the eyes when extra thought (needed to formulate a lie) is required. Finally, technologies are monitoring facial movements, called microexpressions, in the same way poker players watch their opponents for "tells."

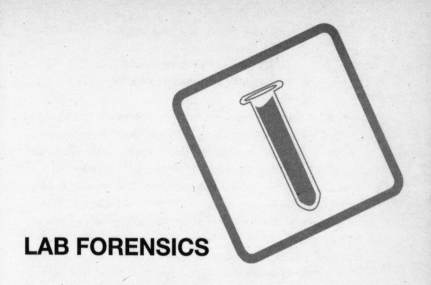

LAB FORENSICS

Who wrote the first forensics textbook?

A lost book written in the sixth century by a celebrated Chinese doctor named Hsu Chich-Ts'si is believed to have been the first to deal with the subject of forensics. An existing work, written by Sung Tzuh in 1247, is thought to be the second.

Who gave the first lectures in forensics?

In the 1640s, at the University of Leipzig, Germany, Johann David Michaelis gave lectures on forensic medicine.

What did the inventor of the Bunsen burner do for forensics?

Robert Bunsen's burner, which everyone who has been to high school used at one time or another, was a product of one of the most important developments in forensic science. In 1859, Bunsen, a chemist, joined Gustav Kirchoff, a physicist, to demonstrate that the colour of the flame produced by a substance can tell you what it is. The pair went on to develop the first spectroscope, which captured light produced by the flame and used a prism to break it up into the component colours unique to the particular elements that produced it. The invention helped forensic investigators learn the composition of materials with small samples, so more could be preserved as evidence.

Why is poison so rarely used as a murder weapon today?

Poisoning has been around for as long as kings, queens, and rivals in love have been plotting against each other. In the nineteenth century, the practice enjoyed a surge in popularity as motive and opportunity collided when insurance policies appeared and household poisons for use in the garden or for controlling vermin became widely available. That prompted new laws designed to make poison more difficult to get, and better science to detect it so police could make arrests. Poisoning is not often chosen as a means of murder today because common poisons are easily detected during an autopsy. However, some poisoners are more inventive, using stimulants and muscle relaxants, or chemicals like ricin and polonium, to ensure that detection remains a challenge.

Quickies
Did you know ...
• that toxins used by poisoners include antimony, arsenic, belladonna, botulinum toxin, copper sulphate, cyanide, hyoscine, lodestone, mercury, muscle relaxants, polonium, ricin, stimulants, thallium, and many more?

How was Alexander Litvinenko poisoned?

A British resident, a former Soviet spy, and a critic of Russian president Vladimir Putin, Alexander Litvinenko died in August 2006 in a very unusual way. He was poisoned with a radioactive material called polonium 210. The poison sent him to an unpleasant and lingering death, which no doubt pleased those responsible. It also had an unfortunate side effect: since his death, hundreds of people — hospital and restaurant workers, airline passengers, people suspected of carrying or administering the poison — became ill or tested positive for radiation exposure.

What is trace evidence?

This is the small, inconsequential stuff. Fibres from clothing, hair, paints and coatings, soil, and pollen are all examples of trace materials that have yielded important evidence.

How can paint chips help police find a hit-and-run driver?

Paint chips can go a long way to narrowing down the list of suspect cars following a hit-and-run accident. They can provide the car's colour, make, model, and year. If police recover the car, investigators can examine it for signs that someone attempted to paint over the accident damage and compare paint chips from it with those found at the scene of the crime.

What keeps some forensic specialists busy with a fibre diet?

Fibres are a type of trace evidence collected at crime scenes. Alone, fibres are not likely to get a conviction, but they can be helpful in tying a suspect to a victim or place. Criminals are likely to leave fibres behind on anything they touch or brush against while committing their crimes. Forensic fibre specialists determine if fibres are synthetic or natural, identify their colour, and, perhaps, pinpoint the clothing, carpet, or piece of linen they came from. Specialists will also look at the number of fibres and how they were distributed around the crime scene to gain insight into the kind of struggle that might have taken place.

When would Prince Charming be the right choice to investigate a crime scene?

Footprints in the garden, a boot print in the snow, or bloody tread marks in the hallway can all go a long way towards tracking down a Cinderella gone wrong. He will make a plaster cast of the print in the garden, use a special spray to preserve the print in the snow, and lift the hall prints with gel, chemicals, or by dusting with powder, like fingerprints.

What does SICAR have to do with footwear?

SICAR (Shoeprint Image Capture and Retrieval) is computer software for storing information about shoes and car tires. It allows forensic investigators to compare evidence gathered at various crimes or crimes scenes, and can be tied into databases of shoe and tire brands and styles. A partial print from a running shoe played a large part in the conviction of David Scott Hall for the brutal murder of a Sault Ste. Marie, Ontario, woman in 2000.

Shoes and tires can incriminate in other ways. Forensic experts can often analyze telltale materials from the crime scene picked up by the treads.

How did the Unabomber frustrate and mislead police?

Ted Kaczynski, the Unabomber, knew investigative techniques very well, and used that knowledge to frustrate the FBI for many years. One of his tricks was to use untraceable recycled materials to build his pipe bombs, which led investigators to call him the "junkyard bomber" at one point during the manhunt. Another thing he did was wear shoes that had the soles of smaller shoes glued to the bottom, so police, analyzing his footprints, would waste time looking for a smaller man.

Where do we find data recorders?

Data recorders are well known on aircraft, and they are also found on trains and ships, but did you know that cars have them as well? In recent years, event data recorders, or EDRs, have become standard equipment on many vehicles. They control things like airbags and restraint systems. Crash investigators can look at them for information on speed, braking, and the severity of the crash. They can even determine if the driver was wearing a seatbelt.

How do identity kits work?

Hugh C. McDonald, a civilian working with the Los Angeles Police Department, developed the identity kit concept in 1940. The kits contained a selection of pieces that represent many variations on facial features such as eyes, ears, nose, and lips. Witnesses combine these to create a picture of the suspect. In recent years, many police forces have replaced them with computerized kits that offer a vast selection of facial features, often of photographic quality. Identity kits can save time and allow police to get a drawing of a suspect out even when sketch artists are unavailable.

What does a forensic artist have to do besides draw well?

Forensic artists have to conduct effective interviews with victims and witnesses who are upset, nervous, and scared to get the answers needed to produce a portrait of a suspect that is as accurate as possible. Their sketches may be hand-drawn, created from an identity kit, or developed on a computer.

Profiling requires an investigator to consider all aspects of a crime. A profiler must:

- study the criminal's actions;
- look for patterns;
- analyze behaviour for insights into the criminal's character; and
- provide a description of the suspect.

Some forensic artists also do facial reconstruction work or sketches of a dead person's face.

Who invented criminal profiling?

London police doctors Thomas Bond and George Phillips are credited with developing a psychological profile of a serial killer, based on a determination that the person responsible for the Jack the Ripper murders had to have had medical training. In another step forward, a psychoanalyst named Walter Langer developed a profile of Adolf Hitler in 1943. His profile rightly pointed out that Hitler would commit suicide if he was defeated. A further milestone in profiling was achieved by James Brussels, who correctly predicted the personality of "The Mad Bomber of New York" in 1947.

Why did psychological profiling fail with the Washington Sniper?

Profiling took a hit during the search for the Washington (also known as Beltway) Sniper in October 2002. Misleading eyewitness testimony and preconceptions about the characteristics of serial killers led the police to spend a lot of time searching for a white van driven by an angry or unstable middle-aged white man, when the killers were, in fact, a former Marine and a teenager, who were both African-Americans.

Why does printing still trip up criminals?

Two teenagers, Nathan Leopold and Richard Loeb, kidnapped and murdered Bobby Franks, the fourteen-year-old son of a Chicago millionaire, in 1924. They thought theirs was the perfect crime, but they were proven wrong when an investigator successfully tied a typed ransom note to some of Leopold's schoolwork.

Typewriters continued to betray criminals right up to the 1990s. Since then, they have pretty much slipped into oblivion, but the usefulness of the signature marks left by machines that turn out printed documents remains. On a laser printer, the giveaway might be a mark on the drum that repeats itself on every page. On inkjets, analysis of the ink can yield brand names and dates of manufacture, the latter being especially useful in identifying forged documents. If implemented, some new technologies could allow investigators to track any document back to the specific laser or inkjet printer that produced it.

BIOMETRICS

What was one of the first uses of fingerprints?

William James Herschel, a colonial bureaucrat in India, is thought to be one of the first people to note the value of fingerprints when, in the late 1850s, he examined those of his own family. Some years later, he insisted pensioners in his jurisdiction provide them as proof of their right to their pensions.

Where were fingerprints first used to identify a murderer?

The first person convicted of a crime by fingerprint

evidence was Francesca Rojas, an Argentine woman who murdered her two children in 1892. She left a thumb-print in blood on a door that matched perfectly with the one taken from her by a police researcher, Juan Vucetich. When confronted with the evidence, Rojas confessed and received a life sentence.

How reliable are fingerprints?

Like everything else in police work, fingerprints are not absolute, but providing they are collected and analyzed properly, they are very compelling pieces of evidence. Defence lawyers will usually attack them by criticizing the matching process.

These days, the accuracy of fingerprint matching processes is coming under greater scrutiny because checks are done so routinely, for everything from terrorist watch lists to traffic stops to job applications. In addition, fingerprint collections are huge. The United States now has about 500 million prints on file, making misidentification a greater possibility, especially if only one finger is used.

Why are prints often said to be latent?

Latent means hidden and *patent* means obvious, although today *latent* is often used to refer to any print on a surface, invisible or not. True latent prints are found with special techniques like powders, chemicals, or lights that make them visible. A third kind of fingerprint, plastic prints, are found on gelatinous materials like grease, soap, wax, or putty.

How do investigators reduce the area that needs to be searched for fingerprints?

Many fingerprints at a crime scene are likely to be latent prints, invisible to the naked eye, because of the type of surface that was touched or because of attempts made to clean up after the crime. Various types of light, including lasers and ultraviolet, can quickly reveal whether invisible fingerprints or other evidence exists, saving investigators a lot of time.

Why do super cops use superglue for fingerprints?

Superglue fuming is a technique used to make latent fingerprints visible to the naked eye. It works because a component of the glue called cyanoacrylate bonds with sweat residue. Fuseo Matsumur, a Japanese trace evidence examiner, received credit for discovering the technique in the late 1970s when he made a mistake while preparing a slide for examination under a microscope.

What are the different fingerprint patterns?

Fingerprints have three basic patterns: arches, whorls, and loops. Most people have arched ridges, about a third have whorls, and loops are uncommon. On their own these catagories are inadequate to make a positive match, so when comparing prints, the centre, called the "pattern area," is examined for line types that further contribute to its uniqueness. Distinctive line types include spirals, bifurcations, and islands. Centre points of sweat glands, ridge path deviation, and the exact end points of islands are examples of very small features, called "minutiae," that also receive consideration.

What piece of evidence freed one of the men arrested for the Great Train Robbery?

In 1963 Britain, fifteen men, dubbed the "Hole in the Wall Gang," pulled off one of the boldest robberies of all time. The Great Train Robbery netted them £2.3 million, close to $50 million today, but not before the train's engineer was injured when he was clubbed over the head.

Though the robbery succeeded, within a few weeks, police arrested thirteen suspects, and twelve got lengthy prison sentences, many mainly because of latent finger-prints on a Monopoly game, beer bottles, and a ketchup bottle left at the farmhouse that served as their hideout. Lawyers for the suspect who got off were able to convince the jury that his prints, which were only on the Monopoly game, could have been there before the game was brought to the farm.

How have fingerprint databases evolved?

Fingerprints used to be stored on index cards in cities, towns, and villages across North America, making them useful for catching local criminals, but not much else. In the early 1970s, the FBI decided a nationwide system was needed to catch a more mobile generation of thieves, so it devised the first fingerprint database. Called the Auto-mated Fingerprint Information System (AFIS), this data-base has since been replaced in the United States by the Integrated Automated Fingerprint Information System (IAFIS). In Canada, the RCMP is installing a system called Real Time Identification (RTID), which will share infor-mation with the American system.

What human characteristics are unique besides fingerprints?

Fingerprints continue to be the most reliable way of determining a person's identity, but many other body parts are receiving consideration as well. The front-runners are the retinas of the eyes, though irises are of value, too. Then there are voiceprints, hand size and shape, footprints (as unique as fingerprints), blood vessels in the wrist, and the distribution of prominent facial features like the eyes, nose, and mouth.

This kind of biological information, along with fingerprints, is increasingly being stored on computers and imprinted on plastic cards or used in devices that scan anyone entering a growing number of countries, organizations, and events. It is the new world of biometric identification.

How useful is voiceprint analysis?

Ideally, voiceprints are unique to individuals, just like fingerprints. In practice, voiceprints have qualities such as pitch that change depending upon the person's mood and circumstances, while fingerprint ridges are with the person for life. For these reasons, when a suspect's voice is to be compared with a voice recording from a 911 call or an investigation, she will be asked to repeat the words several times so the analyst has a range of tones to compare to the evidence. Currently, debates rage in courtrooms on the validity of voiceprint samples because these uncertainties provide room for error.

BLOOD

How is blood evidence collected?

Wet blood is wiped up with a sterile cloth, preferably gauze, dried, and then refrigerated. If blood has dried on clothing or a small object, the investigator wraps it in clean paper, places it in a paper bag, and puts it into a container. If objects are too big to go to the lab, the blood is scraped off onto a piece of paper, which is folded up and placed in an envelope. Samples need to reach the lab quickly; specimens more than forty-eight hours old are probably useless.

How do you read blood spatter marks?

Blood spatter can help reconstruct what happened at a murder scene, if it is read correctly. For instance, circular marks mean the blood dripped straight down or spurted straight out. A blood spurt suggests damage to an artery. Smeared blood means the person or object that made the mark is also bloody. Blood trails show movement. Blood pools show the victim was stationary for a while.

High-speed spatter suggests a gunshot wound, medium speed suggests a knife, and low speed is typically a sign of blunt force.

What made 1901 a big year for blood analysis?

When two boys went missing on a small island off the coast of Germany, a carpenter, Ludwig Tessnow, became a prime suspect. He had been seen with them earlier and clothes found at his house were stained with what he said were wood dyes. An investigator remembered that Tessnow was questioned a few years earlier in relation to a murder with a similar MO that took the lives of two little girls. During that interview, Tessnow had used the same explanation for stains on his pants, and there was no way to disprove his story.

Quickies
Did you know ...
- that in the 1930s a Scottish pathologist named John Glaister listed six ways to classify blood spatter: drops, splashes, pools, spurts, smears, and trails?

By 1901, however, blood analysis had taken a huge step forward thanks to Paul Uhlenhuth, a biologist who had developed tests to distinguish primate blood from other substances. Uhlenhuth's analysis of the stained clothing proved human blood was present. Tessnow's execution took place a few years later.

How does blood type narrow down the suspect list?

Karl Landsteiner, an Austrian pathologist, developed blood typing in 1901. He came up with four distinct types: A, B, O, and AB. Almost three-quarters of people are type O. A and B are each found in 10 percent of the population. Only 4 percent of people are AB. While knowing the blood type of a sample does not solve the crime, it does eliminate many potential suspects and is easy to do.

How did blood spatter and handwriting evidence undo Graham Backhouse?

A bizarre plot by an English farmer to cash in on an insurance policy he had placed on his wife ended with his neighbour dead, his wife maimed for life, and the farmer self-mutilated and under arrest. The blood spatter evidence that unravelled the plot showed that his neighbour could not have cut Backhouse in a struggle as he claimed, pointing instead to the conclusion that he had cut himself. The handwriting evidence against him was the impression of a doodle on a threatening note that had been stuck to the head of a sheep mounted on a fence. Forensics matched the impression to a drawing found on a writing pad in his house.

What are luminol and fluorescein used for?

These chemicals find blood even if the crime scene has been cleaned. Investigators spray them on areas where blood is suspected. If luminol is used, bloodstains glow in the dark. Fluorescein shows stains when UV light shines on the area. Both chemicals react with iron in the blood's hemoglobin.

BODIES

**When did medical evidence begin
to gain acceptance at criminal trials?**

In 1850, a high-profile trial found John Webster, a professor at Harvard Medical School, guilty of killing and
dismembering a wealthy Bostonian named George Parkman following an argument over an unpaid debt. Pieces
of Parkman's body were discovered in a toilet in Webster's
laboratory. Dental records helped establish his identity.

Why do many words about killing end with *-cide*?

Quickies
Did you know ...

- that there are many ways to describe the act of murder, including iced, offed, clipped, burned, broke an egg, did a piece of work, hit, popped, bumped off, put out a contract on, whacked, dispatched, liquidated, took out, wasted, gave a one-way ticket, knocked off, finished, rubbed out, snuffed, chilled, cooled, and dusted off?

Homicide, fratricide, suicide, regicide, infanticide — all these words (and more) get their get their murderous intent from the Latin suffix *-cide*, which means "kill." Another word of recent origin, coined in 1944 to describe the unspeakable horrors of the Nazi concentration camps in the Second World War, was *genocide*, which adds the Greek prefix *genos-*, meaning "race" or "tribe."

What was Julius Caesar's contribution to forensics?

On March 15, 44 B.C., Julius Caesar, emperor of Rome and a lover of Cleopatra before Mark Antony, died at the hands of Roman senators he trusted, including his friend Marcus Junius Brutus. In the world's first recorded autopsy, a physician named Antistius examined his body and discovered twenty-three stab wounds, concluding that only one, through the heart, caused Caesar's death.

What evidence does the body provide of time of death?

Many things happen to a body in the forty-eight hours after death. Muscles began to stiffen within thirty minutes, and a cloudy film develops over the eyeballs in three hours. The core temperature drops about 1.5°F (1°C) per hour. Blood pools at the body's lowest points within about six hours. The body takes on a ghoulish greenish tint after two days. There is stuff to learn inside too. For instance, if the small intestine is empty, death was at least eight hours after the last meal.

What is the difference between a medical examiner and a coroner?

Medical examiners and coroners are found in both Canada and the United States. In the U.S., medical examiners are doctors or forensic pathologists; coroners, on the other hand, are elected and do not require any specific training. Four provinces — Alberta, Manitoba, Nova Scotia, and Newfoundland — use medical examiners, who go out to the crime scene to investigate. Ontario's coroners are appointed and must be licensed physicians. The remaining provinces also use appointed coroners. Unlike medical examiners, coroners do not go to the crime scene. They rely on reports from other death investigators.

How does a pathologist know that a suspected drowning victim actually drowned?

When a person drowns, they usually inhale water into their lungs. If water is absent, the pathologist will begin to suspect some other cause of death. One possibility is dry drowning, where a victim dies from a spasm of the larynx or cardiac arrest before inhaling water. If dry drowning did not occur, the person was probably dead before they went into the water.

Quickies

Did you know ...

- that a coroner's toolkit contains scalpel, bone cutters, scissors, forceps, handsaw, brain knife, chisel, and heavy needle to sew up the body?

What can teeth say about a dead person?

Forensic odontists provide surprising insights about the dead simply by looking at their teeth. By examining wear on the teeth from brushing, they may figure out whether the person was left- or right-handed. The quality of the dental work can identify the person as rich or poor. Teeth will also tell if the person smoked or did a certain type of work — playing certain musical instruments, for instance — that pulled teeth out of alignment.

Another task for odontists is bite mark analysis. Bite marks can be distinctive because of teeth misalignment, damage, or absence. Matching a mark found on a victim or object at the crime scene with an impression of the suspect's teeth has contributed to several high-profile convictions.

How did dental work catch the woodchipper murderer?

On November 19, 1986, in Newtown, Connecticut, Helle Crafts was supposed to pick up her sister-in-law. She did not show up. At first, her disappearance was treated as a missing person problem, but her husband Richard's inconsistent stories about her and a report about some large holes in the couple's living room carpet raised suspicions, even though Richard passed a lie detector test. Eventually police acquired a warrant and searched the house, finding some of Helle's blood. Then police learned that Richard had purchased a woodchipping machine just before Helle disappeared, and a snowplough operator had seen him using it by the side of the road in the middle of a snowstorm on November 20. When police searched the roadside they found an intact letter addressed by Helle, as well as bits of bone, a couple of teeth, a fingertip, blonde hair, pieces of clothing, and five drops of blood. A cap on one of the teeth enabled forensics to match it to Helle's dental records.

Quickies
Did you know ...
• that identity clues include scars, birthmarks, tattoos, implants, dental work, fingerprints, medical records, details of clothing and jewellery, bone fractures, DNA databases, criminal lists, documents like passports, and missing persons lists?

What do skeletons tell
forensic anthropologists?

Dead men do tell tales, even when the flesh is gone. Bones can tell a person's height, age, and gender. They reveal whether the person was healthy and what they ate. Bumps, nicks, and brittleness point to diseases, accidents, or the trauma of the crime, and the skull provides the foundation for very accurate reconstruction of the person's face.

What has to be done to fingerprint
a dead person?

Rigor mortis sets in quickly after someone dies, and one symptom is hand clenching, which makes fingerprints difficult to obtain. To get prints, the pathologist has to pry the hand open by pressing down on the knuckles or by making little cuts in the fingers.

How did forensics experts play a role after
the 9/11 attack on the World Trade Center?

Following the biggest mass murder in U.S. history, a major challenge was naming the 2,749 people who died. Traditional forensic techniques for attaching an identity to human remains, such as fingerprints, dental records, and examination of skeletons proved useful in only a fraction of the cases.

Less than three hundred complete bodies have ever been found. Generally, forensics teams have had to work with fragments of bone and pieces of flesh from one victim that were often closely intermingled with similar remains of other victims. Standard DNA analysis helped provide identification in about four hundred cases, but most of the time, the remains had been subjected to so much heat and crushing pressure that the DNA was unusable. To identify more victims, DNA amplification techniques were developed and other types of genetic testing were conducted. Even so, more than five years into the testing, barely 60 percent of the victims were identified, and the remains of many more wait for advances in the technology.

When are flies good for crime solving?

Forensic entomology is the craft of studying the insects that find a dead body a good place to live. Among the beetles, wasps, moths, ants, and flies, three in particular — blowfly, cheeseskipper, and lesser housefly — are useful in determining time of death, because they conveniently appear at different times during the body's decomposition. Blowflies lay eggs within hours of death. Knowing where the flies are in their life cycle and the temperature of body, an entomologist can make a good prediction of the time of death.

BULLETS

How did ballistics get started?

A French criminal anthropologist named Alexandre Lacassagne noted in 1889 that similarities existed between bullet markings and the rifling grooves cut into a gun barrel to cause the bullet to spin, improving its accuracy. Almost a decade later, in Germany, Paul Jesrich, a forensic chemist, used a microscope to compare two bullets, and in 1925, Philip Gravelle and Calvin Goddard invented the comparison microscope, which made matching much easier and faster.

What is a ballistic fingerprint?

Ballistic fingerprints are lines and indentations left on a

bullet after it has travelled down the barrel of a gun. When a gun is found that might match a bullet from a crime scene, it is fired several times at gel designed to simulate human tissue or into a water tank. The crime scene bullet and the test bullets are then viewed under a comparison microscope to find similarities.

Today, the bullets will also be scanned into a computer and stored in a database that automatically compares them to bullets found at other crime scenes.

How did ballistics figure in the St. Valentines Day Massacre?

The St. Valentine's Day Massacre, pulled off on February 14, 1929, by members of Al Capone's gang in Chicago, clearly showed rival gangs that he meant business. Although no one was convicted of the crime, ballistics analysis of machine gun bullets and cartridges found at the scene was able to rule out police involvement, which had been suspected because three of the hit men wore police uniforms.

Why can cartridges be more desirable than bullets for forensic purposes?

Like bullets, cartridges are marked during the firing

Many factors can make ballistic fingerprinting unhelpful in an investigation. Among the problems:

- mass production means that new guns may be almost indistinguishable from one another, leading to lots of false positives;
- older guns change over time as the barrels wear down and rifling grooves fill up with metal and powder deposits;
- excessive heat can alter a gun's fingerprint;
- bullets may be too badly damaged or fragmented; and
- the user can change the barrel, creating a new gun in the process.

process. Unlike bullets, cartridges do not get flattened, squashed, bent, or broken, so they are easier to examine. Also, cartridges are not affected by a change in the gun barrel because the distinctive markings come from the firing pin and ejection mechanism.

What was DRUGFIRE?

The FBI's DRUGFIRE database helped police identify guns used for multiple drug and gang crimes anywhere in the United States. Developed in the early 1990s, it enabled police to take a gun found at a crime scene, test it, and quickly compare images of its bullets and cartridges to others used in thousands of crimes across the country.

Forensics Technology, a Canadian company, developed a competing spent ammunition database called IBIS (Integrated Ballistics Identification System) in 1996. Through the 1990s, Canadian police and the U.S. Bureau of Alcohol, Tobacco and Firearms (ATF) used that system.

Why were DRUGFIRE and IBIS replaced?

DRUGFIRE and IBIS could not share data. In 2002, they were replaced in the United States by the National Integrated Ballistics Information Network (NIBIN), which solved the compatibility issues and updated the technology. NIBIN focuses on crime scenes, but some states have insisted that the results of test firings of privately owned guns be included as well.

Canada has recently replaced its IBIS system with the Canadian Integrated Ballistics Identification Network (CIBIN). CIBIN will talk to NIBIN, so police forces in both countries can benefit from a larger storehouse of data.

What is a powder burn?

A powder burn may be left on a victim if the gun is fired at close range, for instance, in a suicide. There will be soot and there may be marks called "tattooing," which are left when powder is embedded in the skin. Some burning will exist even if the gun is fired at a distance, caused by heat generated by the bullet while it rapidly spins through the skin. Chemists familiar with explosives analyze the powder residue to determine how it was manufactured and what the weapon was designed for.

What is the connection between the Mafia and Superman?

George Reeves, the actor who played Superman on TV in the 1950s, died from a gunshot wound to the head in 1959 that police said was suicide. Suspicion has lingered since that the case was not investigated thoroughly enough, and that Reeves had ties to organized crime that may have led to his demise. Allen Coulter, director of the *Sopranos* TV series, released a movie called *Hollywoodland* in 2006 that attempted to explore these accusations.

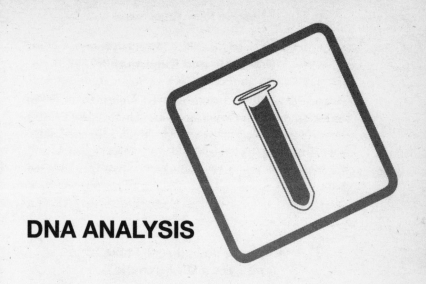

DNA ANALYSIS

Who developed the first DNA profiling test?

Most of the DNA molecule is identical from human to human, but it was the little bit that wasn't that led Professor Sir Alec Jeffreys to design the first DNA profiling test in 1984. The first person convicted by Jeffreys' discovery was Colin Pitchfork. He received a life sentence in 1988 for murdering two teenaged girls in the United Kingdom.

Who was Karen Price?

The Karen Price investigation was a landmark case for both forensic reconstructors and DNA analysts. Karen's body was discovered in 1989 under the patio of a home in Cardiff, Wales. She had been murdered nine years earlier. A reconstruction of her face was made from her skull. When it aired on a TV program called *Crimewatch*, a call came in saying the picture looked like Karen. Her parents were contacted to obtain a DNA sample that was tested against some extracted from the skeleton, yielding a positive match that police were able to use to justify a murder investigation.

How long does it really take to analyze a DNA sample?

Testing times have been getting shorter with improvement to techniques, and accuracy is better too. Nonetheless, analysis still takes at least a couple of weeks and can easily run into many months because of backlogs.

How much DNA is needed for analysis?

A very small amount of deoxyribonucleic acid, or DNA, about one–forty-millionth of a drop, is needed to conduct analysis. Collecting that much is often easy for an investigator, as just a single hair (root included) or a spot of blood may be adequate.

However, the tests are destructive, so the sample must

be large enough to allow some to be kept aside for use in the court and by the defence should they want to conduct their own tests.

How many people in Canada and the United States are free because of DNA?

As much as DNA has been a boon for police, it has also provided tremendous benefits for many wrongly convicted people. One who stands out in Canada is David Milgaard, who gained his freedom because his DNA did not match evidence taken from the body of a raped and murdered woman named Gail Miller. Ultimately, Larry Fisher, who had already served time for several sexual assaults, was found guilty of the crime. Another whose case received a lot of attention was Guy Paul Morin. In the United States, DNA has helped clear about two hundred people.

What is junk DNA?

Very little of the strand that makes up a DNA molecule is actually used to give us our identifying characteristics. The rest is called junk DNA because it has no known purpose. Portions of the junk DNA are the parts of the molecule that get analyzed today.

How is DNA evidence received in court?

The DNA sample produced in court is not absolute. The test might say for example that the odds are a million to one that the accused committed the crime. While that is compelling, the defence is sure to point out that in a country like Canada, with 33 million people, that means the DNA in question could belong to at least thirty-two other people. So while DNA evidence is very helpful, additional evidence is needed to get a conviction.

Under ideal conditions, where a sample is obtained voluntarily at a properly equipped medical facility, the results of DNA testing will be irrefutable. Not so if the sample comes from a crime scene. Samples collected this way are likely to be small, leaving little opportunity to redo tests, damaged through decomposition, or mixed with DNA from others.

MISREPRESENTATION

What makes a cheque legal?

The days of writing a cheque on a scrap of paper are gone. Such cheques lack security features and banks will not want to see them. Midway through 2007, cheques used in Canada needed to be electronically readable, as well.

How are handwriting impressions analyzed?

Many would-be signature forgers have had their plots undone by a 1978 invention called the electrostatic detection apparatus (ESDA). When someone writes on a pad of paper, an impression, however faint, is created on the sheets

Handwriting is analyzed by:

- examination with the naked eye or a magnifying glass;
- shining a light on a slant to look for pressure marks that indicate tracing;
- shining light through the paper to expose eraser marks or correction fluid; and
- comparing inks with a spectrograph or infrared microscope.

below. The ESDA is used to make these impressions visible. A piece of plastic film is laid over the sheet of paper and a vacuum pulls everything tight. The film is electrostatically charged, and the charge changes where indentations exist on the underlying paper. Toner is then applied, and if all goes well, the handwriting appears. Finally, a sticky plastic film is placed over the image to protect it.

What makes a currency attractive to counterfeiters?

Paper money that lacks security features to thwart modern colour copiers is a magnet for counterfeiters. The machines easily make very visually convincing reproductions. The only way to combat them is to introduce a host of features they cannot reproduce, like ink that changes colour depending on the angle of the light, microprinting, letters created with ink that only appears when the money is copied, iridescent ink, and holograms.

Why are American dollars the favoured currency for counterfeiters?

Counterfeiters like currencies that people are not too familiar with but will accept anyway. American dollars are used all over the world, and people outside the United States may not know what to look for to ensure they are genuine.

Credit cards are popular targets for fraud for the same reason. Thousands of companies offer credit cards, making it impossible for anyone to be sure that a card is real by appearance alone.

Who was Elmer Irey?

Working in the U.S. Treasury Department to recover unpaid taxes, Elmer Irey, the "silent investigator," led investigations of tax dodgers and gangsters like Al Capone. From 1928 to 1931, his "T-men" figured out the difference between what Capone was making and what he was reporting to the U.S. government. They then put him in jail for the difference, something police had not been able to do for the crimes of murder, extortion, and bootlegging that he was alleged to have sanctioned.

Irey also played a part in tracking down Bruno Hauptmann, who was convicted for kidnapping Charles Lindbergh's son, Charles Augustus. He traced marked bills in the ransom.

Over his career, Irey tracked down almost $500 million (equivalent to several billions in today's dollars).

What is a forensic audit?

America's multi-billion-dollar Enron case and Canada's $100-million federal sponsorship scandal are examples of illegal activities brought to light by forensic auditors. These investigators search a company's accounts for evidence as though it was a crime scene, looking for information to use in court. In the Enron case, forensic auditors found accounting irregularities that led to charges against Enron Corporation, the accounting firm Arthur Andersen, and some senior executives from both firms. The subsequent meltdown of Enron cost investors and former employees billions of dollars. Arthur Andersen continues as a pale shadow of its former self.

Since Enron and a few other well-publicized cases, pre-emptive forensic auditing has become more common. These kinds of audits are not designed to find crime so much as to identify opportunities for crime before someone tries to take advantage of them.

What is provenance?

Provenance is the story behind a work of art or a col-
lectible. It is information like
where it was made and by
whom, when it was bought
and sold, and whether it was
damaged or repaired. A work with good provenance, like
evidence with a good chain of custody, is likely to be genuine. A work without provenance or with unverifiable provenance can easily be stolen property or a forgery.

Who was the first person prosecuted under RICO for racketeering?

Made law in 1970, RICO (the U.S. Racketeer Influenced
and Corrupt Organizations Act) was brought in to fight
the Mafia. The first conviction, against Frank "Funzi"
Tieri, a New York crime boss known as the "Old Man,"
came ten years later. Other Mafiosi who fell afoul of RICO
included Paul Castellano, who was being prosecuted under it in the 1980s but was killed before the verdict when
he showed up for a meeting organized by another crime
boss named John Gotti. Gotti was later convicted under
the statute, as have been Wall Street traders, motorcycle
gang leaders, rappers, terrorists, antiabortion activists,
and email spammers.

In 1999, Canada did not have an equivalent law, so the federal government relied on provisions of RICO to launch a lawsuit in the United States against several tobacco companies that it said were conspiring with other groups to smuggle cigarettes into Canada.

LEGALESE

When is evidence not accepted in court?

Evidence that helps the search for truth will be admissible in court. Judges do not allow evidence that they think is irrelevant to the case, misleading, or unfairly obtained.

What kinds of paperwork are generated in an investigation?

Paperwork is unavoidable for the police. Courts demand it and investigations are simplified by it. Apart from the investigative reports of the responding officers and detectives, victims need incident reports for their insurance companies, warrants need written requests, evidence has to be tracked with property reports, and lab tests have to be ordered. As an investigation proceeds, additional reports will justify continuing it or recommend closing or suspending it. Superiors may also add reviews and recommendations to what can become boxes upon boxes of paper.

Why is a criminal record called a rap sheet?

Rap sheets predate rap music and have nothing to do with it. The term has more to do with the original meaning of rap, as in "a knock," which by the eighteenth century not only meant rap on something but rap on some*one*, as in "rap the knuckles." This new sense of the word led to slang terms like *bum rap* and *beat the rap*. Although *rap sheet* was probably used much earlier, the phrase did not appear in print until the 1960s.

What goes into the case file?

The case file goes to court to help the prosecution, so it begins with pages that summarize the case and point to key parts of the file that can be used against the accused. The file will also contain testimony from interviews and interrogations, rap sheets, information gathered at the crime scene, and documentation showing how evidence was handled (chain of custody).

What does a New York mayor who became a hero for his leadership in New York after 9/11 have to do with crime-fighting?

During the 1980s, Rudy Giuliani, then a New York district attorney, gained fame for bringing down some organized crime figures and successfully prosecuting Ivan Boesky and Michael Milken, two Wall Street moguls, for insider trading. He logged 4,152 convictions and only 25 reversals. As mayor, he worked against corruption in New York's private garbage removal business and the Fulton Fish Market.

What is the Civil Remedies Act?

It is a law recently enacted in Ontario that allows the Attorney General's office to freeze, seize, and take property used in the commission of crime or bought with the profits of crime. A house used as a marijuana grow op in Oshawa was the first item confiscated under this measure.

How does cross-contamination happen?

The frustration is palpable when a piece of evidence key to the prosecution's argument is shown to have been improperly collected or stored. Hundreds of hours of police and legal work can go down the drain because an investigator left a boot print or fingerprint on latent evidence. To limit the possibility of cross-contamination it is important to define the scene, set up a command post to control who goes in and who comes out, decontaminate any equipment going in, and ensure investigators are wearing their disposable personal protective equipment, or PPE.

What is the prosecutor's fallacy?

Forensic science rarely provides conclusive evidence of guilt, but results of tests are often presented that way in court, even though they really only eliminate segments (albeit large ones) of the population. In the extreme, a DNA test may result in an expert conclusion that only one in a billion people could match the profile. From the prosecution's point of view, that appears to be slam-dunk proof of the suspect's guilt. From the perspective of the defence, however, it is a prosecutor's fallacy, a clear admission that, in a world of 6 billion, any one of six people, including the suspect, could have committed the crime, and without statements from the other five, the prosecution, lacking additional evidence, has no case. The true benefit of the test is that it shortens the suspect list so that police can focus resources more effectively.

How did the most popular Great Train robber go back to jail?

Several of the men involved in the Great Train Robbery of 1963 managed to escape, including Ronald Biggs, who became something of a folk hero in Britain in the 1970s. After escaping, Biggs went to Australia, where he was joined by his wife and children. After a few years, police tracked them to Melbourne, and he escaped to Brazil, leaving his wife behind. In Brazil, he had a child with a girlfriend and needed money, so he tried to sell his story to British newspapers. In 1974, the *Daily Express* offered him £35,000, but someone there also told Scotland Yard how to find him. Biggs was arrested but beat extradition back to Britain because of his Brazilian-born child. In 2001, several strokes caused him to ask Britain to let him come home where he could get free medical care. His request was granted, but he had to resume serving his sentence.

A judge can rule evidence inadmissible for a variety of reasons, including:
- the statement is hearsay;
- the claim lacks foundation;
- the witness is speculating;
- the statement is irrelevant;
- the evidence is immaterial; or
- the witness is not an expert.

Where was the world's longest criminal trial?

A trial in Osaka, Japan, against Etsuko Yamada, a female teacher accused of murdering two mentally impaired children, began in 1978 and concluded in 1985 with a not guilty verdict. When the death of former Serb President Slobodan Milosevic on March 11, 2006, ended his war crimes trial four years after it began, it became the longest war crimes trial in history. The Nuremburg trials of Nazi war criminals lasted just ten months. Canada's Air India trial ended with an acquittal after more than a year. The longest U.S. trial lasted twenty-nine months.

What happens if the police know who did it but cannot prove it beyond a reasonable doubt?

We have all heard of known criminals getting off on so-called technicalities, and it makes us wonder whether law enforcement and justice officials can adequately protect us. The simple answer is they cannot. Some guilty people will go free because we have committed to try to protect the innocent. Police usually comfort themselves on this point by remembering that criminals will continue to offend and will eventually be convicted. Of course, when murder or assault is involved, this is really no comfort at all.

How is bail determined?

When someone is arrested and held in Canada, they have a right to appear before a judge within twenty-four hours, unless released sooner, for a "show cause" hearing. At the hearing, the prosecution explains why the person should be held or, in special instances, the person explains why they should be released. The judge then determines how high bail should be set.

How many countries insist on proof of guilt "beyond a reasonable doubt"?

A formula put forward in the 1700s by William Blackstone, an English jurist, that says, "better that ten guilty persons escape than that one innocent suffer," has become the foundation of criminal law in English-speaking countries and has gained broad acceptance internationally. Nonetheless, many parts of the world still presume a defendant guilty unless he can prove his innocence.

In the face of threats from terrorists who, given a chance, will send suicide bombers to indiscriminately slaughter hundreds of people, the idea of having the justice system wait until the event happens is unacceptable. Conversely, proactively jailing would-be terrorists for contemplating such deeds — for thought crime — is also repugnant in a free society.

What is wrong with vigilante justice?

Vigilantes operate alone or in groups to watch for threats to their community ("keep vigil"), seek revenge, or fill a hole they think exists in the justice system. They get in trouble with the law when their strikes against the individuals or groups they do not like are planned or premeditated rather than committed in self-defence. Even non-violent vigilantes like the Guardian Angels are viewed skeptically by many people who feel that vigilantism is a step down the slippery slope towards lawlessness.

Who stops crimes against the environment?

The more appropriate question might be who *tries* to stop crimes against the environment. Incidents of poaching, pollution, illegal logging, and animal trafficking are increasing in scale and number all around the world; the penalties continue to be weak; the "good guys" like customs agents, the Coast Guard, conservation officers, and special police detachments are stretched too thin; and the burden of proof is high.

Who was Adolph Beck?

Adolph Beck had a key role in bringing about an appeals system in Britain, but not in a way that gave him any comfort. In 1895, he was convicted of a crime he did not commit in a complete travesty of justice. Twenty-two women he was alleged to have taken money and valuables from identified him in a poorly constructed physical lineup in which he was the only grey-haired man. To make matters worse, the judge ignored or disallowed evidence that could have helped him, while allowing an unverified claim that he had committed similar crimes in 1877 under the name John Smith. Released in 1903, Beck was soon re-arrested when a woman complained that he had defrauded her. While he stewed in jail awaiting his next trial, police picked up another man for committing similar crimes. Ultimately, this man, who looked a lot like Beck, confessed to the current crime wave and to the crime waves in 1877 and 1895 that put Beck behind bars in the first place.